GH00858995

Vegetable Soups for the Soul

Enough Recipes to Get You through a Year of Colds and Aches

by Chloe Tucker

License Notes

Table of Contents

Introduction

When was the last time you felt down? It was a couple of months ago, or perhaps you're going through a rough patch right now. Whether it's a cold or heartbreak that's got you under the covers, a warm bowl of soup always makes you feel better. However, we're skipping a chicken soup this time around and are giving you a collection of vegetable soups to get you through any physical or emotional rollercoaster life may throw your way.

We know you're not feeling your best, so we've made sure our recipes are quick and easy because while cooking doesn't necessarily make everyone feel better, the washing that comes after NEVER helps anyone get better. When you think about it, we're kind of like your fairy godmothers. We're here when you need us, and we're here to help. Unfortunately, we haven't been gifted with fairytale magic to have the soups make themselves while you're in bed, so we're going to need a little bit of your help with this.

The trick to any good soup is a high-quality stock or broth as its base. Without it, the soup can be rather bland and even watery. With not much else but boiled ingredients going on there, a watery soup is any cook's nightmare! And, when you're already feeling under the weather, we know it doesn't take much for you to cry of desperation or want to throw stuff against the wall, so we've designed these recipes to be anything but watery.

With all that out of the way, we think you're ready to start. Take it easy and go at your own pace; there's no need for you to chop like Gordon Ramsay or roll out special orders like in Ratatouille, alright? It's just a vegetable soup for you. You're at home, just trying to take care of yourself, so if one carrot's bigger than the other or the onion isn't perfectly diced, no one's telling on you. Just take a deep breath and make the soup one step at a time, the way life should be dealt with. After all, whether it takes you 30 minutes or 2 hours to make, it's still the vegetable soup for the soul. Good luck!

Recipe 1 - Cabbage Soup

Duration: 30 minutes

Serving Size: 8

List of Ingredients:

- Olive oil- 3 tbsp.
- Onion- ½
- Garlic cloves- 2
- Water- 2 quarts
- Chicken granules- 4 tbsp.
- Salt- 1 tsp.
- Black pepper- ½ tsp.
- Cabbage head- ½
- Tomatoes- 14.5 ounces

|||||||||||||||||||||||||||||||||||||||||||||||||||||||||||||||||||||||||

Preparation:

Heat the oil in a saucepan and fry in the onion and the garlic.

Add in the water and the chicken granules.

Now season with salt and pepper.

Chop the cabbage and add to the pan.

Stir in the canned tomatoes and let simmer for a few minutes before serving!

Recipe 2 - Toscana Soup

Duration: 10 minutes

Serving Size: 5

List of Ingredients:

- Sausages- 12
- Oil- 1 tbsp.
- Diced onion- ¾ cup
- Garlic- 1 tsp.
- Chicken soup base- 2 tbsp.
- Water- 4 cups
- Potatoes- 2
- Sliced kale- 2 cups
- Cream- 1/3 cup

IIIIIIIIIIIIIIIIIIIIIIIIIIIIIIIIIIIIIIIIIIIIIIIIIIIIIIIIIIIIIIIIIIIIIIIIII

Preparation:

Bake your sausages in the oven at 300 degrees Fahrenheit until browned.

Chop them.

Add oil in a pot and add in the baked sausages and the onion.

Fry for a few minutes and add in the garlic and the soup base.

Add in the water and the potatoes and cook till they are tender.

Now add in the sliced kale and let simmer.

Finally, add in the cream and then serve!

Recipe 3 - Vegan Broccoli Soup

Duration: 25 minutes

Serving Size: 8

List of Ingredients:

- Cashews- 1 cup
- Vegetable broth- 5 cups
- Potatoes- 2
- Onion- 1
- Broccoli- 4 ½ cups
- Basil- 1 tsp.
- Sea salt- 1 tsp.
- Black pepper- ¼ tsp.

||||||||||||||||||||||||||||||||||||||||||||||||||||||||||||||||||||||||||

Preparation:

Add the cashews and the vegetable broth to a blender and blend.

Take a pot and add the rest of the vegetable broth, potatoes and onion.

Bring to simmer and let cook for a few minutes.

Add the basil and the broccoli and let simmer for 10 minutes till all the vegetables are cooked.

Add the cashew mixture, and add the salt and pepper.

Serve hot!

Recipe 4 - Sweet Potato Chili Soup

Duration: 1 hour

Serving Size: 5

List of Ingredients:

- Vegetable broth- 5 tbsp.
- Onion- ½ cup
- Garlic cloves- 3
- Jalapeno pepper- ½
- Sweet potatoes- 2
- Chili powder- 2 tbsp.
- Cumin- 1 tbsp.
- Paprika- ½ tsp.
- Oregano- ½ tsp.
- Red pepper flakes- ½ tsp.
- Tomato paste- 1 ½ tsp.
- Vegetable broth- 2 cups
- Tomatoes- 1 can
- Kidney beans- 2 cups

||||||||||||||||||||||||||||||||||||||||||||||||||||||||||||||||||

Preparation:

Heat the 5 tbsp. of vegetable broth in a saucepan and add in the onion, garlic and jalapeno pepper until soft.

Add the sweet potato, chili powder, cumin, paprika, oregano and red pepper flakes.

Pour the rest of the broth.

Bring to boil and then let simmer for the potatoes to cook.

Add the tomatoes and the kidney beans and simmer for 45 minutes before serving.

Recipe 5 - Simple Avocado Soup

Duration: 30 minutes

Serving Size: 3

List of Ingredients:

- Homemade vegetable stock- 3/4 cup
- Peeled ripe avocado- 1
- Milk- 1/4 cup
- Chopped coriander- a dash

||||||||||||||||||||||||||||||||||||||||||||||||||||||||||||||||||||||||

Preparation:

In a saucepan, add the vegetable stock and bring it to heat.

Add in the ripe peeled avocado.

Now mix in the milk and stir.

Pour the soup into bowls and garnish with chopped coriander.

Cool it slightly before serving to your baby.

Recipe 6 - Sweet and Spicy Squash

Duration: 10 minutes

Serving Size: 3

List of Ingredients:

- Medium acorn squash- 1
- Sweet apple, peeled and cored- 1
- Melted unsalted butter- 2 tsp.
- Maple syrup- 1 tsp.
- Cinnamon- a pinch
- Nutmeg- a pinch
- Cloves- a pinch

|||||||||||||||||||||||||||||||||||||||||||||||||||||||||||||||||||||||||||||

Preparation:

Preheat your oven to 350 degrees Fahrenheit.

Cut the squash in half and remove the seeds. Cut it in half again.

Place the squash pieces on a greased baking tray with the skins facing up.

Cover them and bake in the oven for 30 minutes.

In a bowl, combine the apple, butter, maple syrup, nutmeg, cinnamon and cloves. When the squash is done, put the apple mixture on top of the squash pieces.

Cover the dish and put it in the oven to bake for about 20 minutes.

The squash can then be pureed or blended in a food processor and served to the baby.

Recipe 7 - Mushroom and Barley Soup

Duration: 25 minutes

Serving Size: 5

List of Ingredients:

- Barley- 1 cup
- Olive oil- 1 ½ tbsp.
- Onions- 2
- Salt and pepper- a pinch
- Carrot- 1
- Celery stalks- 2
- Mushrooms- 20 ounces
- Vegetable broth- 5 cups
- Bay leaves- 2
- Fresh thyme- 2 tbsp.

|||||||||||||||||||||||||||||||||||||||||||||||||||||||||||||||||||

Preparation:

Boil the barley with 4 cups of water.

Heat oil in a pan and add the onions, salt and pepper.

Now add the carrot and the celery and cook for few minutes.

Add the mushrooms, broth, bay leaves and thyme and let simmer for 10 minutes.

Mix in the barley and cook.

Discard the bay leaves and serve!

Recipe 8 - Carrot, Cabbage and Potato Soup

Duration: 30 minutes

Serving Size: 6

List of Ingredients:

- Sliced carrots- 4
- Sliced potatoes- 2
- Sliced onion- 1
- Sliced cabbage head- ¼
- Garlic cloves- 2
- Chicken stock- 6 cups
- Olive oil- 1 tbsp.
- Dried thyme- ¼ tsp.
- Dried basil - ¼ tsp.
- Dried parsley- 1 tsp.
- Salt- 1 tsp.
- Ground black pepper- a pinch

|||||||||||||||||||||||||||||||||||||||||||||||||||||||||||||||||||

Preparation:

Add the sliced potatoes, onion, carrots, cabbage head, garlic, olive oil, chicken stock, dried thyme, dried parsley, dried basil, salt and black pepper in a saucepan.

Mix all the ingredients.

Bring it to a boil and let it boil for a few minutes.

Reduce heat to low and let simmer until the carrots are cooked and the cabbage is tender.

Cool the soup mixture.

Once cooled, pour the mixture into a blender and blend in all the ingredients to make the soup.

Pour into bowls and serve hot!

Recipe 9 - Vegan Hot and Sour Soup

Duration: 30 minutes

Serving Size: 6

List of Ingredients:

- Mushrooms- 1 ounce
- Lily buds- 12
- Water- 2 cups
- Bamboo fungus- 1/3 cup
- Soya sauce- 3 tbsp.
- Rice vinegar- 5 tbsp.
- Cornstarch- ¼ cup
- Tofu- 8 ounces
- Vegetable broth- 1 cup
- Red pepper flakes- ¼ tsp.
- Black pepper- ½ tsp.
- White pepper- ¾ tsp.
- Chili oil- ½ tbsp.
- Sesame oil- ½ tbsp.
- Onion- 1

||||||||||||||||||||||||||||||||||||||||||||||||||||||||||||||||||||||||||

Preparation:

Place the mushrooms and the lily buds in hot water to make them tender.

Drain and reserve the liquid.

Cut the mushrooms and the lily buds.

Soak the bamboo fungus in another bowl in hot water with salt.

Blend the soya sauce, rice vinegar and cornstarch. Put half of the tofu in this mixture

In another saucepan, add the vegetable broth and the lily buds and mushroom and bring to boil.

Add red chili flakes, black pepper and white pepper.

Mix cornstarch and water with the soup mixture.

Mix the soya sauce and the tofu mixture and let simmer.

Add the bamboo fungus, chili oil and sesame oil.

Garnish with green onion and serve.

Recipe 10 - Easy Vegetable Beef Soup Recipe

Duration: 3 hours

Serving Size: 16

List of Ingredients:

- Lean beef- 2 pounds
- Mixed vegetables- 4 cans
- Tomatoes- 4 cans
- Chopped onion- 1
- Black pepper to taste
- Salt to taste

||||||||||||||||||||||||||||||||||||||||||||||||||||||||||||||||||||||||

Preparation:

In a large pot, cook the beef for a few hours until soft and tender.

Drain the liquid and now add in the vegetables, tomatoes, onion and let it simmer for 3 to 4 hours.

Season with salt and pepper before serving.

Serve with prawn crackers.

Recipe 11 - Tuscan Soup

Duration: 20 minutes

Serving Size: 4

List of Ingredients:

- Chicken broth- 6 cups
- Chopped onion- 1
- Italian sausage- 9 ounces
- Potatoes- 3
- Spinach- 1 bunch
- Evaporated milk- ¼ cup
- Salt- a pinch
- Black pepper- a pinch

‖‖

Preparation:

Crumble the sausages and fry them in a frying pan.

Now add in the chopped onion and cook for a few minutes.

Transfer to a large pot and add in the potatoes and the chicken broth.

Add in the spinach and cook until the potatoes are cooked.

Remove from heat and then add in the evaporated milk, salt and pepper.

Serve!

Recipe 12 - Vegetarian Black Bean Soup

Duration: 25 minutes

Serving Size: 4

List of Ingredients:

- Olive oil- 1 tbsp.
- Onion- 1
- Celery – 1
- Carrots- 2
- Garlic cloves- 4
- Chili powder- 2 tbsp.
- Cumin- 1 tbsp.
- Black pepper- a pinch
- Vegetable broth- 4 cups
- Black beans- 4 cans
- Corn- 1 can
- Tomatoes- 1 can

||||||||||||||||||||||||||||||||||||||||||||||||||||||||||||||||||||||

Preparation:

Heat oil in a pan and fry the celery, onion, carrot and garlic for a few minutes.

Add cumin, chili powder and black pepper.

Add the vegetable broth, 2 cans of black beans and corn and boil it.

Blend the remaining black beans and the tomatoes in a blender and add in the soup mixture and simmer for a few minutes.

Recipe 13 - Spicy Kimchi Stew

Duration: 45 minutes

Serving Size: 5

List of Ingredients:

- Sesame oil- 1 tbsp.
- Beef- ¾ cup
- Water- 3 cups
- Soya sauce- 1 tbsp.
- Chopped scallions- 2
- Chopped garlic cloves- few
- Chopped onion- ½
- Kochukaru- 1 tbsp.
- Kochujang- 1 tbsp.
- Kimchi- 2 cups
- Cubed tofu- 1/2 cup

||||||||||||||||||||||||||||||||||||||||||||||||||||||||||||||||

Preparation:

Stir fry the beef in the sesame oil; now add the kimchi and fry it.

Add the garlic, onion, kochukaru and kochujang and mix.

Now add the water and let it cook for 30 minutes.

Add the tofu after a while and, in the end, add the scallions.

Recipe 14 - Super Soup

Duration: 15 minutes

Serving Size: 7

List of Ingredients:

- Turkey legs- 2
- Diced celery- 1 cup
- Potatoes- 1 ½ cups
- Cream of chicken soup- 20 ounces
- Cheese- 1 pound
- Diced carrots- 1 cup
- Diced onion- 1 cup
- Chopped broccoli- 16 ounces
- Water- 4 cups

‖‖‖

Preparation:

Boil the turkey legs in the water.

Chop the meat and add it to the broth again.

Now add in the diced celery, potatoes, diced carrots, diced onion and chopped broccoli.

Cook for a few minutes, then add in the cream of chicken soup.

Add in the cheese and let simmer until the cheese has melted.

Serve!

Recipe 15 - Cabbage, Potato and Parsnip Soup

Duration: 20 minutes

Serving Size: 20

List of Ingredients:

- Cubed potatoes- 3
- Parsnips- 2
- Vegetable bouillon base- 2 tbsp.
- Water- 2 quarts
- Salt- a pinch
- Pepper- a pinch
- Applesauce- 1 cup
- Balsamic vinegar- 2 tbsp.
- Garlic cloves- 3
- Truffle oil- 1 tsp.
- Chopped green cabbage head- 1

||||||||||||||||||||||||||||||||||||||||||||||||||||||||||||||

Preparation:

In a saucepan, add the parsnips, cubed potatoes and the vegetable bouillon base.

Add the water and cook the vegetables until they are cooked and tender.

Add in the salt and the pepper.

Cook for 15 to 20 minutes.

Cool the cooked vegetables.

Once blended, add the vegetables to the blender and blend in all the ingredients.

Once the vegetables are pureed, pour them back into the saucepan and simmer for 5 minutes.

Now add in the balsamic vinegar, applesauce, garlic paste and truffle oil and stir.

Let simmer for a while before adding the chopped cabbage head.

Cover and cook until the cabbage is cooked and soft.

Serve!

Recipe 16 - Miso Soup

Duration: 10 minutes

Serving Size: 4

List of Ingredients:

- Dashi granules- 2 tsp.
- Water- 4 cups
- Miso paste- 3 tbsp.
- Tofu- 8 ounces
- Green onions- 2

||||||||||||||||||||||||||||||||||||||||||||||||||||||||||||||||||

Preparation:

Add dashi granules and water to a saucepan.

Let them boil.

Next, add in the miso paste and the cubed tofu.

Let cook for a few minutes.

Finally, chop the green onions and add them to the soup.

Serve hot!

Recipe 17 - Broccoli and Velveeta Cheese Soup

Duration: 10 minutes

Serving Size: 6

List of Ingredients:

- Chopped broccoli- 30 ounces
- Chicken broth- 30 ounces
- Margarine- 6 tbsp.
- Onion- 1
- Flour- ½ cup
- Milk- 2 cups
- Velveeta cheese- 1.5 pounds
- White pepper- a pinch

‖‖‖

Preparation:

Cook the broccoli in a large pan and add in the chicken broth.

In another pan, fry the onions with the margarine.

Add in the flour and milk to form a creamy texture.

Add this to the broccoli mixture.

Now add in the white pepper and the Velveeta cheese.

Cook for a minute.

Serve!

Recipe 18 - Lamb and Barley Soup

Duration: 20 minutes

Serving Size: 8

List of Ingredients:

- Ground lamb- 1 pound
- Chopped onion- ½
- Canned tomato - 28 ounces
- Water- 2 cups
- Beef consommé- 28 ounces
- Condensed tomato soup-10.75 ounces
- Chopped carrots- 4
- Chopped celery - 3
- Barley- ½ cup
- Chili powder- 1 tsp.
- Black pepper- ½ tsp.

|||||||||||||||||||||||||||||||||||||||||||||||||||||||||||||||||

Preparation:

Add the ground lamb, onion and tomato to a saucepan.

Next, add in the water, consommé and condensed tomato soup.

Add in the chopped carrots, chopped celery, barley, chili powder and black pepper.

Simmer for 45 minutes before serving.

Recipe 19 - Red Lentil Soup

Duration: 20 minutes

Serving Size: 4

List of Ingredients:

- Peanut oil- 1 tbsp.
- Onion- 1
- Ginger root- 1
- Garlic clove- 1
- Fenugreek seeds- a pinch
- Red lentils- 1 cup
- Butternut squash- 1 cup
- Cilantro- 1/3 cup
- Water- 2 cups
- Coconut milk- ½ cup
- Tomato paste- 2 tbsp.
- Curry powder- 1 tsp.
- Cayenne pepper- a pinch
- Nutmeg- a pinch
- Salt and pepper- a pinch

‖‖‖

Preparation:

Heat oil in a pan and fry the onion, ginger root, garlic and fenugreek seeds.

Now mix the lentils, squash and cilantro and mix well.

Add the water, coconut milk and tomato paste.

Add the seasonings, cayenne pepper, curry powder, salt, pepper and nutmeg.

Bring to boil and then let simmer till the lentils and squash are cooked.

Recipe 20 - Vegan African Stew

Duration: 1 hour 15 minutes

Serving Size: 6

List of Ingredients:

- Olive oil- 2 tbsp.
- Yams- 3 cups
- Onions- 2
- Cabbage- 2 cups
- Tomatoes- 2
- Flaked coconut- 6 tbsp.
- Garlic cloves- 3
- Tomato juice- 3 cups
- Apple juice- 1 cup
- Ginger- 1 tsp.
- Cayenne pepper- ¼ tsp.
- Salt- a pinch
- Bell pepper- 1
- Peanut butter- ½ cup

||||||||||||||||||||||||||||||||||||||||||||||||||||||||||||||||||||||

Preparation:

Heat oil in a pan and add the onions, yams, cabbage, tomatoes, coconut and garlic for about 7 to 10 minutes.

Put the apple and the tomato juice and add the ginger, cayenne pepper and salt.

Let simmer for an hour.

Now add the bell pepper and the peanut butter.

Cook for half an hour and then serve!

Recipe 21 - Apple and Sweet Potato Soup

Duration: 15 minutes

Serving Size: 2

List of Ingredients:

- Flour- 2 tsp.
- Unsalted butter- 2 tsp.
- Homemade chicken broth- 3/4 cup
- Apple sauce- 2 tsp.
- Cooked sweet potatoes-3/4 cup
- Ground ginger- a pinch
- Ground cinnamon- a pinch
- Milk- 1/2 cup

||||||||||||||||||||||||||||||||||||||||||||||||||||||||||||||||||||||||||

Preparation:

In a saucepan, melt the butter and stir in the flour. Cook until the mixture turns golden brown.

Now add the chicken broth and add in the sweet potatoes, apple sauce, ginger and cinnamon. Bring to boil and let it simmer for 5 minutes.

Blend the mixture into a food processor and transfer it back to the saucepan.

Add in the milk and serve warm.

Recipe 22 - Butternut Soup

Duration: 15 minutes

Serving Size: 6

List of Ingredients:

- Butternut squash- 2 pounds
- Onions- 2
- Butter- 1 tbsp.
- Vegetable broth- 4 cups
- Cream- ½ cup
- Salt- a pinch
- Ground nutmeg- a pinch
- Cloves- a pinch
- Ground cinnamon- a pinch

‖‖

Preparation:

Add the butternut squash, onions and butter to a bowl and microwave them.

Now add in the vegetable broth and cook for a few minutes.

Blend these ingredients together in a blender.

Now add in the cream and the salt and mix.

Next, season your soup with nutmeg, clove and ground cinnamon.

Serve!

Recipe 23 - Simple Broccoli and Cheddar Cheese Soup

Duration: 15 minutes

Serving Size: 4

List of Ingredients:

- Bread slices- 4
- Cheddar cheese- 4 ounces
- Butter- 1 tbsp.
- Garlic clove- 1
- Chicken stock- 1 quart
- Broccoli florets- 2 heads
- Cream- 1/3 cup
- Cayenne pepper- ¼ tsp.
- Salt- a pinch

‖‖

Preparation:

Add the cheddar cheese to the bread slices and, with the help of a torch, melt the cheese.

Put butter in a saucepan and fry in the garlic.

Now add in the chicken stock and the broccoli florets and let them cook.

Season with salt and cayenne pepper.

Add in the cream and mix.

Pour into bowls and serve with the cheese toast.

Recipe 24 - Carrot and Ginger Soup

Duration: 10 minutes

Serving Size: 4

List of Ingredients:

- Butternut squash- ½
- Olive oil- 2 tbsp.
- Onion- 1
- Carrots- 1 pound
- Garlic cloves- 3
- Ginger- 1
- Water- 4 cups
- Salt- a pinch
- Cream- ¼ cup

‖‖

Preparation:

Preheat your oven to 350 degrees Fahrenheit and roast the butternut squash in the oven.

In a pan, add in the oil and fry the onions and the carrots.

Add in the garlic and ginger.

Add in the water and let cook.

Add in the roasted butternut squash.

Blend this mixture in a blender.

Season with salt.

Pour into bowls and serve with cream.

Recipe 25 - Baked Potato Soup

Duration: 15 minutes

Serving Size: 6

List of Ingredients:

- Bacon slices- 12
- Margarine- 2/3 cup
- Flour- 2/3 cup
- Milk- 7 cups
- Baked potatoes- 4
- Green onions- 4
- Cheddar cheese- 1 ¼ cups
- Sour cream- 1 cup
- Salt- 1 tsp.
- Pepper- 1 tsp.

‖‖‖

Preparation:

Fry the bacon slices and crumble them.

In a pot, add in the margarine and the flour and stir.

Add in the milk and the cubed potatoes.

Now add in the bacon slices.

Mix in the cheddar cheese, sour cream, salt and pepper.

Let cook for a few minutes and top with chopped green onions.

Serve!

Biography

For decades, this beautiful actress graced our screens with her incredible talent and performance in movies that captivated the script and emotions of the viewers. Well, life rarely goes as planned, but we should always make the best out of it, like Chloe.

Originally from the bubbly city of Los Angeles, she has moved from the movie industry into the food scene. Her role in Mama Mia ignited her passion for food. She has taken the New York scene by surprise. Charmed by the unique regions she had visited, the delicious delicacies she tasted, her uncanny appreciation for flavors, ingredients, and cooking techniques have continued to wow customers wide and far.

However, as mentioned, she started as an actress. Breaking into the food scene was easy because she had contacts and connections, but satisfying clients was a different ball game. Over the years, she has mastered the food scenes and unique flavors clients seek. Today, her clients can attest to the high-quality food from her restaurants.

The New York food scene is a jungle that only the strong dare to tread. However, she was a passionate student and learned the tricks and tips, and slowly set her passion for delivering excellent tastes to all who sought them.

An Author's Afterthought

Did you like my book? I pondered it severely before releasing this book. Although the response has been overwhelming, it is always pleasing to see, read or hear a new comment. Thank you for reading this and I would love to hear your honest opinion about it. Furthermore, many people are searching for a unique book, and your feedback will help me gather the right books for my reading audience.

Thanks!

Chloe Tucker

Printed in Great Britain
by Amazon